WORDS FROM THE HEART
BY
EARL THOMPSON

WORDS FROM THE HEART
EARL THOMPSON
COPYRIGHT 2012 EARL THOMPSON
FIRST EDITION
ISBN: 978-1-300-01951-0

LOVE IS

Love is an emotion too strong to hide
It can lead you astray; it can be your guide
Love is not selfish, love is kind
Love is something that should always be on your mind
Love is the greatest emotion given to a man
It can take away his weakness, and make him strong
When you love, you have no fear
Except for those for whom you care
Love is gentle, sweet and tender
Love is an emotion to which you gladly surrender
Love builds you up so you see the light
Love is an emotion that feels so right

YOU'RE ALWAYS ON MY MIND

I wish you were here to see
The pain you're causing me
You left without saying a word
It must be my heartbeat that I heard
You were quiet and you didn't say
What it was that was causing you to stray
In my heart I thought I treated you good
But obviously I wasn't doing what I should
I gave you the best years of my life
And you were the best part of me as my wife
But somehow you weren't happy here with me
There were more things that you wanted to see
But you wouldn't let me know
Where you wanted to go
I had loved you with all my heart
And I thought we would never be apart
But I can now see
Your heart is not here with me
Now I wish you all the happiness you can find
And to let you know, you're always on my mind

You Were The Girl Of My Dream

I dreamt yesterday that I saw your face
And you had your usual poise and grace
You stood watching me for awhile
With that rather usual, crooked smile
You watched me and then you turned and walked away
Without even stopping to listen to what I had to say
It was a dream, but I could feel what was happening
And I felt sad as I watched you disappearing
I awoke to find myself alone
It was only an illusion, and I was still on my own
You were the only girl I had in my life
The one I wanted to be my wife
There was no sign that you wanted to go
Why did you leave? I do not know
You were the sweetest person I have ever seen
You were the girl of my dream
You were everything to me
And with you I wanted to spend eternity
You shattered my dream when you went away
I can never forget that terrible day
It was the day my heart was broken in two
The day I was forced to say goodbye to you

You Were My Hope

You were everything to me
My hope, my joy, my prosperity
When I had you
Life was like a dream come true
Everything I wanted I had
Happiness was mine, I was never, ever sad
You were always there for me
And I never wanted to know what life without you
would be
You taught me everything I needed to know
And you told me how far for me you would go
There was nothing you wouldn't do for me
Even lay down your life if need be
Tolerance and patience was your name
And as long as you lived, it remained the same
You never yelled at me when I did things that were
wrong
You took charge and showed me what it was to be
strong
When you died, I knew I had lost the best part of
me
And I knew I'd never find another one like you
through all eternity
I love you and I wish you were here
So that I could once again feel love and genuine
care

Will We Ever Be Together Again

As I sit and watched the days go by
I find I can't stop the tears I cry
I cry because you're no longer with me
The reason is now clear for me to see
I acted like a child when I should have been a man
I was weak when I should have been strong
I trampled on your emotions as if I didn't care
And now, how I wish that you were here
I cry myself to sleep at nights
Hoping when I awake in the morning, things will be right
But it keeps going on and on just the same way
You left me, and that was such a terrible day
I sit here and I wonder where you are
Is it over? Has it gone that far?
Is there a chance for a reconciliation?
Or have I waited for too long?
Can you find it in your heart to forgive me?
Or should I continue through this misery?
Is there a place for me in your heart?
Or will we continue to be apart?
I need you to ease my pain
And to tell me if we will ever be together again

When Love Turns To Hate

I never thought I'd see the day
When we would both go our separate ways
We didn't take advantage of what we had
And at times we treated each other real bad
There were times when I said very poignant things
to you
And there are times when you did the same thing
too
Sometimes I see the tears in your eyes
But I still turn away and wondered why
Why were you acting like a child?
I never realized I was doing things to drive you wild
I never knew I was hurting you so
And now it's time to go
Time to go our separate ways
With now what seem like goodbye being the best
thing to say
Do you think we could start anew?
And do the things that we didn't do
Now that we are on separate sides of the fence
We can see why we used to have all those
arguments
I sincerely hope it's not too late
Let's try once more before we finally separate
Because it really does hurt, when love turns to hate

What is Your Secret?

Is there a secret to your looking so young?
Whatever it is that keeps you that way must be very strong
Is it that you have found the fountain of youth?
Or is it that the life you live is so pure and is filled with nothing but the truth?
You never seem to change as far as I can see
What is it that keeps you this way? Is it a secret or a mystery
If the world could know your secret, then it would be a much more beautiful place
Because everything that is old and ugly would disappear without leaving behind a trace
I can't help but to admire your smile, your beautiful teeth
Is there anything so lovely, so sweet?
You're always looking so fine and is such a sight to behold
This must be a secret, because the half has never been told

You're A Very Beautiful Woman

I looked at you and I could see the tears in your eyes
He has hurt you so badly that you want to cry
He didn't tell you there was another woman in his life
That he was married and still has his wife
He kept pulling you along for the fun of it
And now it hurts you so much when he decides to quit
You ask why did he have to say it to you now?
But it would have come out, someway, somehow
You wanted to know why he didn't say it to you before
Because he was afraid he would have lost you for sure
You're a very beautiful woman and desirable too
He probably has never seen a woman as sweet as you
You fell in love with him, now you'll have to let him go
Or else you'll be hurting a woman you don't even know
Men have been playing these tricks for a long time now
And yet they keep succeeding, someway, somehow
You see, being beautiful has its disadvantages too
Because men will always try to be the first to hurt you
Some men think a beautiful woman will never settle down
Because of her looks, she will always want to play around
But you are not like that, I know for sure
You are a beautiful woman and much, much more

You are intelligent, sensitive and warm inside
You're full of so much love; it's hard to hide
You are gentle, sweet and kind
You're amongst the best women a man could ever find
Give me your hands and you will see
What sweet destiny awaits you and me

Together Forever

If the world were made for only two
Then it would just be for me and you
There's never been two with so much to share
But with us, it was divinely prepared
God puts us here for us to stay
Living together, forever and a day
Each day of our lives, our love will grow
And our feelings for each other will always show
A love like this happens once in a lifetime
And I'm glad that it happens in yours and mine
With all my heart, I do love you
And I know deep inside you feel the same way too

The World Needs Love

The world is crying out for peace
But yet the war they refuse to cease
They are building nuclear weapons
And that can only cause destruction
The world is crying out for justice
But they do bad things for all to notice
They say freedom is what they want
But human bondage is what they chant
They talk about equality
But on top is where everyone wants to be
They say you should not kill
But this is what they are doing at will
Peace and freedom can only be attain through love
Which can only be achieved from the creator above
But until humans acknowledge that He exist
This is what we'll continue to miss
The world needs peace and love
Something that can only be achieved from the creator above

THE SWEETEST GIRL

What kind of a man would leave someone as sweet as you
He must be sick, demented too
As I look at you I see a perfect example of a wife
Someone any man would want in his life
How could he have gone and left you all alone?
Could it be that he couldn't see what he has for his own
He must be one of those guys with wondering eyes
Seeking to get someone else's property, but he is not wise
He has left the sweetest thing back at his home
And has gone out on the street to roam
I wonder what he has on his mind
And what on the street does he intend to find
You are the sweetest girl I have ever seen
How could he have been so mean?
Wipe those tears from your eyes
Let him be the one to cry
Because he has lost something he'll never again find
The sweetest girl who is now mine.

Thank You

I didn't think that I'd ever feel this way
The moment we met, you brightened my day
You brought back the smile that was missing from my face
And made me feel that the world is a wonderful place
Before I met you, loneliness was all I could see
And I thought that the world was a miserable place to be
But you made me feel I have nothing to worry about
And now I'm beginning to fall for you without a doubt
To hear your voice is what I long for each day
And I keep hoping that about me, you feel the same way
You're everything I have ever wanted in a woman and more
And with your love I know I would feel so secure
I hope you can see what you have done for me
You've given me hope in a world full with misery
I thank you for making me feel this way
My world is now looking brighter with each passing day

Someone Like You

I looked in your face and I saw you smiled
And I felt as if my heartbeats stopped for awhile
I have never seen anyone like you
You are the complete image of a dream come true
I don't know where you are from, or where you go
But the meaning of love you must know
There is no better definition to love than you
You are love through and through
I have never seen anyone as lovely as you
Or even as beautiful too
To describe your beauty, there is no word in the
Lexicon
There is nothing I can say for anyone to understand
Someone must see you to know how sweet you are
Your beauty shines as brightly as the morning star
How great the man must feel who has you in his life
You are the perfect example of a wife
He must cherish the very earth you walk on
And probably thinks he is the luckiest man
I think he is lucky too
To have someone as sweet as you
Do you come in pairs
Or is such beauty very rare?
I would like to have someone like you
Someone in my life too

Someone As Sweet As You

If I had you for my wife
I wouldn't want another woman in my life
Because you are everything I want and more
And with you, I'd feel so secure
You wouldn't have to worry about my going away
Because by your side is where I'll forever want to stay
When I saw you for the first time, I didn't know what to say
Just one look at you, made my day
How could any man say his dream has come true?
When he has never met a woman as sweet as you
Surely, you're a gift sent from above
Because when I look at you, all I see is love
A love so pure and true
A love that could only come from someone like you
You're a dream come true
And I'm glad I've met someone as wonderful as you.

Loving You Is All That Matters

Presently loving you is all that matters to me
Yesterday what we had in the past is history
Once in the past we couldn't get along
Everything we did was wrong
I often wondered how is it we said we love each other
When all we did was fight like sister and brother
We just couldn't see eye to eye
And I often wondered why
For us there was such a bright future together
But presently we just couldn't battle that stormy weather
Every time the wind blows, we sank further into the sea
And there was no one there to help either you or me
We were sinking and needed help fast
Struggling, not knowing how long we would last
At times I felt as if I didn't want to be touched by you
And I know you felt the same way too
We knew we loved each other, but what was wrong?
Maybe what we felt for each other wasn't strong
Now with the help of God, we have learned how to love
our blessings are flowing freely from above
Now what I feel for you is true
And I can sincerely say "I love you"
Now our love has truly set us free
And I can say with sincerity
Loving you is all that matters to me

Loving You Is All That's On My Mind

I have special thoughts of you every day
And I know you think of me the same way
You are everything I want in a woman and more
And with your love I feel so secure
This special feeling I have, I have never felt before
And every time I talk to you, it leaves me wanting more
I can't wait to be with you
And to experience a love that is so true
Not being with you is like my worst nightmare coming to past
But I know it won't forever last
Your love is an inspiration to me
And just the thought of you leaves me in ecstasy
Loving you is all that's on my mind
Because you are the sweetest girl a man could ever find

MY FUTURE IN MY PAST

They say you cannot find your future in your past
But when I found you, I found mine at last
You were the woman of my dreams and I didn't know
I was young and stupid, and it showed
I went away leaving you behind
To search for a future I would never find
I didn't know my future was with you
I didn't know you were my dream come true
In my search, I couldn't see
That those other women were not meant for me
But still I try to find one who would understand
The type of man I am
I searched but it was in vain
Because all I could find was heartaches and pain
Then you found me and you were my saving grace
One mention of your name and everything falls into place
How could I have been so blind that I couldn't see
That you were the only one who was meant for me?
And now I feel at peace at last
Because I have found you again, my future in my past

My Love For you

This distance between us will never drive us apart
Each day, my love for you grows stronger in my heart
I pray for the day when you'll always be with me
So I can make you as happy as can be
Though I am far away from you
It's just these precious memories that carry me through
There are days when everything seems to go wrong
But when I think of you, it always makes me strong
I love you more than words can say
And the feeling grows stronger with each passing day
This love I feel for you will always be true
And I hope you think of me in whatever you do
Only time will bring us together and this is true
And in the meantime, I'll always pray for you

My Sweetheart

I don't know where I'd be
If I hadn't met this woman who is so special to me
She has that smile which is so incredibly sweet
And that was the first thing that swept me off my feet
I remembered looking at her as if I were transfixed
And all I wanted to do was to kiss those beautiful lips
Another thing that caught my attention were those beautiful eyes
They had me staring, gaping, completely mesmerised
She has the softest and most delicate voice I have ever heard
I would try to describe it if only I could find the words
As she approached me, I found my knees becoming weak
She softly said "Hi" I tried to answer but couldn't speak
And then she touched my hand
And an emotion swept through me, only I could understand
She gave me the greatest present I could ever want in life
When I asked her, she said, "yes, I'll be your wife."
Since then she has given me the most beautiful child
One I'll treasure for a long while
I can't help but feel how lucky I have been
To be the husband of the sweetest woman I have ever seen
To me, she is the queen of all mates
One who I'll always love and will always appreciate

My World Is Falling Apart

My world is falling apart without you
I can't help it; I don't know what to do
You walked out of my life as if I didn't exist
With not even as much as one kiss
You didn't care what you did to me
But when you left, I became the unhappiest man in history
Every day I asked myself the reason why
But every time I think back, all I can do is cry
I guess I wasn't man enough for you
But you just wouldn't tell me what to do
Every time I look in your eyes, I could see you were sad
But tell me please, was I treating you that bad?
Why didn't you tell me the way you feel?
So I could change my attitude and get real
Then I would have known what to do
To stop this relationship from falling through

My Heart Is In Terrible Pain

Sometimes I wish you were here to see
What your leaving has done to me
I am not half the man I used to be
And I cry at nights from sheer misery
I don't know what I did to drive you away
But obviously sorry is not enough for me to say
I call your name hoping that you will appear
But you are gone forever and that is my greatest fear
I look around trying to see your face
But you have disappeared without leaving behind a trace
Where are you, I asked myself
Are you somewhere being with someone else
The thought is enough to drive me mad
And I am here by myself and feeling very sad
Why did you have to go
This is something I need to know
Because my heart is in terrible pain
And I need to know if I'll ever see you again

ONLY IN MY DREAMS

It happened again last night
I had another dream that I was holding you tight
But then I knew it wasn't true
Because I woke up feeling sad, lonely and blue
I wanted to keep dreaming about you forever
Because only in my dreams can we ever be together
Lately, loving you is all that's on my mind
But to me the world is cold, cruel and unkind
It holds me in its grip and won't let me go
And I can't tell you how much I love you so
All I can do is imagine you being with another man
And trying hard to understand
Why it wasn't I who was that close to you
Why it wasn't I who was your dream come true
You're the sweetest girl I ever know
And for you my love continues to grow
If it were not for my imagination, I wouldn't know
what to do
Because that's the only way I can ever be with you
In my mind I continue to love and cherish you
But in reality there is nothing I can do
For you, I'd give my very life
If I could have you one day for my wife
But for me, this will never be
Because you're only of my dream, not my reality

OUR GRACIOUS AND LOVING FATHER

Our gracious and loving Father up above
Teach us your wisdom and your love
Help us as we go along each day
And let us be mindful of the things we say
Teach us how to be helpful to our sister and brothers
And how to be kind and loving to each other
You send your Son who died to show the way
And for this, we're thankful each and every day
We know that without your love, we can't go on
We know that only your love can keep us strong
We are mindful that you're the one who keeps us alive
And we thank you for each day that we survive

Let Me Be

There were times when I thought I was free
But what is this that's happening to me?
I can't be who I want to be
People are always trying to change me
I want a life that's best for me
But this they refuse to see
They want me to change from who I am
They want me to be a different man
I don't know what I'm supposed to do
I can't work for my dreams to come true
They don't understand me
It's like they want me to be in captivity
I often wonder what they want from me
And why they won't let me be
But sometimes it's hard to see
That the way I am, is the way I want to be
I can't help whatever is happening to me
But I won't be the man they want me to be
I'll forever remain this very same man
Because I know for me, God has a plan

JESUS IS MY ROCK

Jesus is my Rock, of this I'm sure
For me He has opened the glory door
He is everything I'd like to be
For His love has saved me from my miseries
Jesus is the King of my life, and this I see
Because He is always there for me
He'll never leave me when I'm down
For me he'll always be around
Jesus is my Rock and my salvation
He leads me away from the world's temptation
He'll forever be there to see me through
Because His love is so pure and true
He is the Gift that was sent from above
The one who shows us what it is to love
He showed me love when there was none
And now my life has just began
Jesus is my Rock; He is everything to me
He is my Lord and Saviour; He has set me free
He is the King of my soul, and this I know
I will serve Him forever, wherever I go

I Still love You

Tears fell from her eyes as she watched him go
Why did he leave, she didn't know
She had been the best wife she could be
And he had promised her eternity
He told her he wouldn't go, no matter what the circumstance
But now he is leaving without giving her a second chance
She didn't know what changed his mind and made him decide to go
All she knew was that she loved him so
He was very good to her and then he just changed
And started doing things that were very strange
He would come in late at nights
And with her he would pick a fight
She was doing the best she could
But for him that just wasn't good
He would accuse her of having an affair
And told her she just didn't care
He said he was doing the best he can
And she was there cheating with another man
She told him it wasn't true
But to convince him, there was nothing she could do
Things got from bad to worse
And he changed from a loving husband to one resembling a curse
But still she was sad when he packed and walked out the door
And knew that this was the end of the relationship for sure
How poignant it is to say goodbye
When you don't know the reason why

He was her life and though the relationship was
through
She whispered, "I still love you."

Heaven Must Be On Holidays

I saw you for the first time and didn't know what to say
Your beauty shines as brightly as the perfect day
I wanted to come closer, but I couldn't move my feet
My eyes have never behold anyone so sweet
You are the most beautiful girl I have ever seen
No wonder in England they are looking for a queen
Because you're here with me, tantalising me
Displaying your beauty so perfect for the eyes to see
I was entranced by such a beauty, and couldn't say a thing
All you need to be an angel are two beautiful wings
I know you have been told that you're a very beautiful girl
And one any man would welcome into his world
You smile and it helps to enhance your beauty
I look at you and an angel is what I see
I wanted to speak but I couldn't find the words
And suddenly it was as if my heartbeats could be heard
Heaven must be on holiday why a beauty like you is on earth
When you were born, the angels rejoiced at your birth
Give me your hands so that I can lift you off the street
You're much too beautiful for the earth to bruise your feet

I DO NEED YOU

Losing you has made me realize
What it is to be sensible and wise
I had you for myself
You were mine and you belong to no one else
But I played around like I was fool
I hurt you and I broke all the rules
I was never around when you needed me
I stayed away leaving you in misery
You always wanted to show me how you feel
But I ignored you, telling you to get real
I didn't know I was doing wrong
I thought that I was macho, and was being the perfect man
At times I saw you sitting by yourself
Acting as if you were alone, and there was no one else
Instead of reassuring you that I was there
I stayed away as if I didn't care
How I wish that you were here again
So that I could reassure you and ease your pain
My pain is such that it's hard to bear
I didn't know it could be so poignant when you care
Now I know what you were going through
And I am hoping you will tell me what to do

I'll Be That Perfect Man

Why did I stay away so long?
I guess I didn't understand
That for emotional support, you needed me
But I was like a child and I couldn't see
That what I was doing was wrong
But still it made me feel like a man
I was hanging out with the crowd
And it made me feel very proud
It made me feel as if I were in control
But I didn't know that I was being blatantly cold
I ignored you when you called my name
To me it was as if you were playing a game
I acted like I was a free man
When I should have been living up to my obligations
I should have known I was being led astray
I should have listened when you asked me to stay
I couldn't understand the pain you were going through
And I keep on asking myself, what did I do?
Now you are gone and the crowd is no longer appealing to me
They are like a constant reminder of my misery
Losing you has caused me to take a stand
And with you again in my life, I'll be the perfect man

I'LL ALWAYS THINK OF YOU

As time passes, I try to understand
Why you left me for another man
I did everything to make you stay
But still you up and went away
I wasn't the most romantic man in the world
But one thing I know, you were my only girl
I was always there for you
Doing whatever you wanted me to
Still another man came and stole your heart
And I was left shattered and completely torn apart
I thought I was doing everything that's good
But obviously I wasn't doing what I should
You needed love; I gave it to you
But you went away, breaking my heart in two
Whatever you wanted, you could have asked
For you, I'd do even the most monotonous task
I was always willing to go that extra mile
It warmed my heart, Oh! That delightful smile
Now all I can do, is think of you
And imagine another man holding you as I use to
It saddens me; I've lost you for good
Anything I could do to win you back, I would
Just try to reminisce on what we've been through
And in the meantime, I'll always think of you

I'll Be What You Want Me To Be

I'm beginning to think of you again
And the very thought is causing me grave pain
When I was with you, I was the happiest man alive
Now that you're gone, I'm finding it hard to survive
You were everything to me and more
And when I was with you, I felt so secure
But I took you for granted and I couldn't see
That you were slowly, slowly leaving me
I find it hard to sleep at nights because of you
And I toss and turn, not knowing what to do
My friends tell me to be a man and get over you
But it's easier said than done; it's something I cannot do
I wish I had spent more time with you
I wish I had considered the pain you were going through
But happiness made me blind, and I couldn't see
That I was causing you pain and misery
I'm able to see clearly now, and this is true
I love no one else but you
Give me a chance again and you'll see
I'll be just what you want me to be

I Love You Sincerely

Yesterday, I saw the tears in your eyes
But I just couldn't understand why
If you said you are happy here with me
Then why do the memories of him always bring you misery?
You can't seem to get him off your mind
And since lately, you have been crying all the time
It doesn't appear as if I am any comfort to you
God knows I have tried, but I don't know what to do
Our love life is not what it was before
And I'm beginning to think you don't love me anymore
You told me once the memories of him will never hurt you again
But what is this I'm seeing, if it is not pain?
He is with another woman, and I'm sure you know
So why do you keep loving him so?
You're no longer on his mind, I'm sure
'cause where you're concerned, he has closed that door
He no longer wants you in his life
'Cause he has gone and made another woman his wife
Now all I want is for you to be happy with me
'Cause I do love you sincerely

I'll Always Be There

I am no longer sure in you what I see
Is it beauty or is it misery?
You never stay the same
You always seem to change
I can no longer tell whether you're going or coming
I don't know whether you're hurting or loving
You seem to be in a state of confusion
What is it you want? Love or contention?
You don't know whether you are happy or sad
In the past you weren't sure of the things you had
You look at me and you're not even certain about me
And sometimes I wonder if I am the one you see
Sometimes you seem so far away when I call your name
And I wonder if I am not the one to be blamed
You were so happy when you weren't with me
What have I brought to you, is it misery?
Once you were as free as a bird in a tree
Now what have I brought to you, Captivity?
If you want to go
Please let me know
I do love you but your happiness means more to me
I'd rather let you go than to see you in captivity
Though it hurts my pride to see you go
I must let you know
That I still love you so
Goodbye and take care
But remember, if you need me, I'll always be there

I Am The Luckiest Man

I was searching for you but you found me
How we came to be, is a mystery
You came out of a dream into my life
You are so charming, sweet, perfect for a wife
I didn't think that dreams do come true
But I am a living proof, I've got you
I am the luckiest man on the face of the earth
I've got love and all it's worth
Looking at you has made me understand
What real love can do to a man
I was a drifter going away from home
But now that I have found you, I no longer want to roam
Here with you is the happiest place to be
And I want when you wake up, to be the first person
You see

I AM SORRY

When I saw you, I didn't like the way I feel
It was love at first sight, and this was real
I was told that I would fall in love one day
But I didn't believe in this love thing anyway
But now I know that they were right
There really is love at first sight
I didn't like the way I felt inside
This was an emotion I couldn't hide
I told myself that I would never fall in love
Unless it was an angel sent from God above
And there you were, as if you were out of a book
With the cutest smile and the prettiest look
You sent my heart racing wildly in my chest
Of all the women I've seen, you do look the best
You smiled at me and my heart skipped a beat
I've never known anyone to smile so sweet
We talked and made love that night
And oh, how it felt so right
If there were love, it was what I was feeling then
I was scared, and never wanted to feel this way again
I'm a sore loser, and I was losing this race
Things were moving too fast, I couldn't handle the pace
When I woke up, all I could do was flee
Because I couldn't believe that this was happening to me
Since then I realize you're one of a kind
And I can't seem to get you off my mind
Forgive me and accept my apology
I was scared and I'm sorry

HOPE

I don't know where I'd be without Hope
With all the heartaches and stress, it helps me to cope
Sometimes I'm so depressed, I don't know what to do
But when I think of Hope, I see my way through
Stress and heartaches can throw you down
But with Hope, you can stand on solid ground
With Hope you can see your way through the darkest day
Because Hope helps you to feel you can find the way
When you're in despair, Hope can see you through
Because it's the feeling to have when you're feeling blue
Hope can make it seems good when it's really bad
And it can make you feel happy when you should be sad
When you have Hope, you just know what to do
And anxiety and despair won't bother you
Hope can drive you in the path of success
Because it will help you to deal emphatically with stress
Without Hope, I don't know where I'd be
Because my life would be filled only with miseries

Have We Been Lovers Before

As I look at you standing there
I know I have seen you before somewhere
But I can't remember when
Could we have been lovers back then?
I seem to remember that lovely smile
And your very teasing, sexy style
I remember my heart beating this way before
Which tells me I have seen you somewhere for sure
We could have been lovers or even friends
But a part of me must have died when this friendship ends
I grudge the man who has you for his own
You belong to him and that means I'll be left alone
I can't think of being with anyone except you
But you belong to another, and to him you're true
He must think he is the luckiest man in the world
And he has a right to be; he has you for his girl

Happiness

Happiness is a condition of the mind
It's something if you search deep within you'll find
If you don't want to be happy, there is nothing
anyone else can do
Because happiness has to come from inside of you
Happiness can be all around you but you cannot see
Because inside of you there is only misery
Your mind is a powerful thing and this is true
But don't allow it to control you
Search for the happiness that is within you
And work diligently to make your dream come true
Life without happiness is wasted as you can see
Because without it, there can only be misery

Forget About Him

It had never occurred to me
That you were living in misery
I thought that you were happy here
Never thought you'd be better off over there
Where you can see him every day
As he goes along his merry way
I thought it was over between you two
But now I can see that it isn't true
You just can't seem to get him off your mind
Is he the best thing you could ever find?
You know he can see you as he passes by
But this way he will never turn his eyes
You mean nothing to him at all
If you continue this way, you're sure to fall
For any man you would make a beautiful wife
Forget about him and live your life
Over him you're losing your sleep
But he has someone else's love to keep
He has another woman keeping him warm
But you're dying for him to come into your arms
If you seek, a better man you will find
And with help, you can drive him out of your mind
He isn't worth crying over
Right beside you is a man dying to be your lover

FORGIVE ME

Are you really leaving me?
I'm pleading desperately
Look into my eyes
Do you see the tears I cry?
I cry because of the way I feel
Because I can't believe you're leaving for real
I really did think I was being good
But probably I wasn't doing the things I should
They say it takes a man to admit he's wrong
But if I were a man, I would have been strong
Right now all I feel is desperation
And I'm trying sincerely to understand
Why would you want to leave all we have behind?
Is there something better out there that you find?
The world has nothing to offer but sadness and pain
Can you really afford to throw away all we have gained?
Is there no chance for reconciliation?
Or is it that what I've done is so terribly wrong?
Look into yourself and take a look at me
The man you say you'll love endlessly
He is still standing here before you
With a love that is so true
Forgive me, I beg of you
And there is nothing I wouldn't do
To stop this relationship from falling through

CHRIST CAME

The dawn of this day
Came in a very special way
There were no dark clouds in the sky
And they all wondered why
Things have not been good of late
And there was for this special thing that they wait
Is this the day they have been waiting for?
Or would they have to wait for much more?
Everyone waited with great anxiety and anticipation
Would this be the end of their tribulation?
Would someone really come to ease their pain?
So that they would be free to roam again?
The prophets have been prophesying about this day
And there were some very special things they say
That a king would come to set them free
And save them from all their miseries
They said that Jesus was to be His name
And that it would forever remain the same
But a Humble Man came along that day
And they didn't look His way
He preached about the kingdom of God
And told them to follow Him and give away all they had
Everyone was looking for an earthly King
But who was this man, and what did He bring?
All He had was the word from His mouth
And hardly anyone listens to what He was talking about
They thought that He was blaspheming Himself
So they didn't listen to Him, they were expecting someone else
And His followers were the ones who were hurt
When He gave His life and all it was worth

A Lost Soul Remembering His Love

Is there ever any one as lovely as you
With eyes so bright, and so delightfully blue?
Your beauty is like something that reaches the heart
And I pray constantly to God that we won't forever be apart
Every time I remember those eyes, it's sheer nostalgic
And I can't help but feel lonely and terribly sick
Being away from you is like my worst nightmare coming to past
And I can't help but wonder how long it will last
I stare constantly at your picture as if I am hoping for it to come to life
And I hope and pray for that day when you'll be my wife
It's only you in my thoughts that keep me alive
The memories of those wonderful days together that helps me to survive
How longer must I live without you?
How longer must I go on feeling lonely and blue?
These are questions I keep asking myself
Only you can answer, no one else

A Mother's Cry

Oh lazy child, can't you see?
The pain and distress you're causing me
I have to work hard so that you can eat
Yet you're too proud to remove these shoes
from my tired feet
I sweat and toil to make ends meet
So that I can keep you off the street
But all you do is sit and eat
With the coffee table as cushion for your feet
You never make the bed you sleep in at nights
And you turn on but never turn off the lights
You sleep constantly and think that that is cool
And you are always complaining whenever
you're to go to school
You don't know the significance of an education
And you are much too lazy to understand
That it was just because I was as lazy as you
Why I am now suffering as much as I do

A SMILE

A smile is a powerful thing
There is so much joy that it can bring
A person may feel his world is at an end
But a smile can show him that he has friends
A smile is better than a dollar or two
Because a smile can do so much for you
A dollar or two will soon disappear
But the memories of a smile can last for years
A smile can say the things words cannot say
A smile can help to brighten your day
Keep smiling as you do the things you do
And watch as someone smiles back at you

ALWAYS MEMORIES

I had that dream again last night
The one in which you promise to make things right
But then you just up and went away
And I haven't seen you since that day
I cry myself to sleep at nights
Because I'm not allowed to hold you tight
How could you love me and treat me so bad?
I have memories, but they always make me so sad
What can I do to win you back to me?
Should I continue to live on these memories?
All that I have of you is a picture on the wall
A constant reminder of why I gave you my all
I gave my very heart to you
But you went away, breaking it in two
How can I love someone else without a heart?
You stole it from me, and now we're apart
I wish that you could see
What your leaving has done to me
Memories are not enough to carry me through
I want you back in my life, 'cause I still love you

A Wife's Cry

My husband is a writer, my daughter is too
Sometimes I'm so worried, I don't know what to do
They both daydream all day long
And between both, I can't get a single thing done
My husband is always writing
My daughter sits around the computer, typing
They are always writing poems and stories too
I hope one day that their dreams will come true
Around the computer, my husband has a special seat
And sometimes I simply get the inclination to compete
But I guess I have to stick to what I know
So off to work I go

A PRISONER'S PLEA

Here where I'm living is sheer hell
So many things happening, half of which I can't tell
I had so many dreams, which just shattered in front of me
Now loneliness and darkness are all that I see
I was happy and had a good life when I was free
But I was foolish; drugs took a hold of me
Now I'm looking at a world, which was once mine
A world I will never again find
I know you're out there in someone else's arms
And getting what is rightfully yours, a man's charms
When I had you, I ignored you all the time
Looking somewhere else, and not at what was mine
Now my world is so terrible without you
And there is absolutely nothing I can do
In my world I get up every day and have a bite to eat
And then I go back to being on my feet
There are so many of us in here, it's a crime
All of us paying for our mistakes, doing our times
I was weak, but I just wouldn't listen to you
When you said my friends were bad, I said it wasn't true
They brought drugs into my life
And for that I ignored even you, my wife
And now I can't stop hearing your voice
Constantly telling me, I had made the wrong choice
I had made the choice to stay with my friends
Not knowing it would lead to my untimely end
Tell me that there is a place for me in your heart
And maybe it will be easier for me to make a new start
I'm here hoping you'll forgive me

And save from my miseries

Get Rich Much Faster

I look around and I don't know what to say
Why are the churches so obsessed with money these days?
At church, all they talk about is money, money, money
It's getting so scary; it's not even funny
It seems like we're paying for salvation
On top of all these terrible taxation
It's getting so that nothing is free anymore
Now we're paying for what Christ did two thousand years before
The pastors are getting away with murder, so to speak
They're making thousands and thousands each week
Some churches ask for a week salary comes Easter
It's like we're giving nothing to God, everything to Caesar
I said I'd become an entertainer to get rich quick
But my friend looked at me as if I were sick
He said you don't know what you're saying
Go to church and look at all the tithes they're paying
If you want to get rich quick, become a pastor
I'm sure you'll get rich much faster

A LOVE THAT IS PURE AND TRUE

Another day has passed and I haven't seen your smiling face
Now I know why everything is going at such a slow pace
You are not here and everything is as dreary as can be
And for me, it's hell, sheer misery
I didn't know that longing for someone could be so poignant
But now I'm sure that you're the one that I want
When I'm home, I can't help but to think of you
And it makes me sad when I don't know what to do
Most of my days are lonely and blue
And it's even more so when I can't see you
For some reason, when I see you, my spirit soars
And I don't feel as lonely and as terrible as I did before
I have special thoughts of you every day
And my wish is that you feel the same way
If I had you in my arms, I'd be as happy as can be
Please tell me how to win your love for me
I feel something very special for you
And I hope you feel the same way too
This feeling I have is only for you
And I know it's a love that is pure and true

THE POLITICIANS OUT THERE

There are Politicians out there that I hate to see
Because they're causing anger, pain and misery
They watch callously while people die
Then they turn their backs and give a pleasing sigh
They pretend to be in charge
But they present a better picture of lunatics at large
In public, they pretend they will ease our pain
But in private they do things to increase the strain
They tell us to hold our heads up high
But they will do nothing to help our children who cry
They tell us our country we should be proud to die for
And so they go out and create wars
They tell us they would one day make peace
But the war they refuse to cease
The world is getting so corrupt, it's a crying shame
With these people in charge playing head games
They play tricks on our minds
And tell us things will be better in time
They do things to turn us against each other
And watch as brothers kill brothers
Election times, they make promises to the poor
And when they win, these promises they ignore
They try to make us understand
That it is wrong to give a helping hand
People of a different race
Are made to feel out of place
The world is falling apart
Because there no love left in man's heart

YOU ARE MY WORLD

I sat here reminiscing on the day we met
It is one that I'll never forget
You came out of a dream into my world
A sweet, sincere, yet shy girl
You are everything I've always dreamed about
And when I saw you, in my mind there was no doubt
For me, life was going to be good once more
You are the girl of my dream, of this I'm sure
You are everything I have ever wanted in a girl
And it was like you were from a different world
You smile and it brightens your very face
It was as if you were not of the Human race
When God created you, an angel was what He had in mind
Because you're the most beautiful girl a man could ever find
Your voice is as soothing as a Violin
And when you speak, it reaches the very heart within
Your face is as bright as the Morning Star
And it reflects how sweet and delightful you are
I cannot begin to tell you what you mean to me
But the world have eyes, and with them they'll see
You are the best thing to ever happen in my life
And I'm proud that I have made you my wife
You are the picture of love
A gift that was sent from God above
You are my world, my little darling dove

YOU ARE THE LOVE OF MY LIFE

I look at you and I fall in love over and over again
And with you my entire life I would like to spend
I have never seen a woman I could love more each day
But you have filled that capacity in every way
You are the most caring person I have ever known
And for you more and more my love has grown
It touches my heart to see you smile
And I feel like staring at your face all the while
You have the most soothing voice I have ever heard
And to describe it would be much too hard to find the words
There is no greater incentive in life than to be with you
And holding you in my arms forever is what I want to do
In whatever I do, you're always on my mind
You're the sweetest woman a man could ever find
You always have the nicest things to say
And whenever I'm sad, you continually make my day
Loving you is the greatest thing to ever happen for me
And I said this with all sincerity
You're the love of my life
The woman I have made my wife

I REMEMBER THAT TERRIBLE DAY

I sat and watched another day go by
And I found that I still want to cry
I still remember sitting here watching you
And there was nothing I could do
I remember your constant sufferings and your pains
And you calling out my name over and over again
I remember you looking at me with tears in your eyes
And asking the question, why
Why did it have to happen to me?
Why was I afflicted so severely?
You had made a pledge to stay with me forever
And now that you're gone, we're no longer together
I remember sitting beside your bed day after day
And to comfort you, there was nothing I could say
I remember watching your body rocking with coughs
And how painful it was when I couldn't hear your laughs
I watched you as your whole body deteriorates
And asked myself, was this to be your fate?
You had given so much to life
But you didn't live long enough to be my wife
We spent a short time together before you became ill
And I remember watching you, feeding on those pills
But they didn't do a thing to help you
If anything, it was more pain that they put you through
When you died, I drank my sorrows away
And to join you one day is for all that I pray
I will always remember that terrible day.

MY FOREVER VALENTINE

Honey, there is something special I'd like to say
I thank God that we have lived to see another valentine's day
But here is something even more special, and it's true
I thank God for the day that I found you
You've been an inspiration throughout my life
And I'm so thankful that you've made me your wife
I love you more and more as the days go by
And no one can separate us, no matter how hard they try
I know that you're my lover, and you'll always be mine
And I want you to be MY FOREVER VALENTINE
Te Quiero, mi amor

Jamaica, Land For Which My Heart Yearns

Jamaica, land of my forefather and of my birth
how longer must I go on feeling this pain and this hurt
I've been away from you for so many years
now I'm feeling lonely and engulfed by my fears
Fears that I may never live to go back home
fears that I'll always continue to roam
When I remember your warmth and your beauty
I can't help but to bring back to mind my sincere promise
and my bound duty
A duty to return one day to your soil where I can once again be free
Free to enjoy your warmth and tranquillity
But it seems I'll never come back home to you
and I feel lost, afraid and miserable too
It seems as if my dreams will die here with me
because there is no way out that I can see
My problems I can only share with myself
because to understand me there is no one else
I long to sit on your shores where I can freely meditate
and watch as all my problems levitate
What a day that will be when I should return
to a land for which my heart so much yearns

MY DEAR MOTHER

Mother, you have taught me all I need to know
And that is why I love you so
Since birth, you've always been there for me
Showing me all the things I needed to see
Still, I know I wasn't the best son
But I thank you for all that you have done
There were times when you could have walked away
But despite the odds, you still chose to stay
There were times when things weren't going right
But still you chose to stay and fight
Sometimes I watched as you endured terrible pains
But, mother, your sacrifices will not go in vain
You've taught me how to be brave and strong
And you've made me an independent man
It's because of you why I'm still alive
And why I'll always continue to thrive
You're the best mother there could ever be
And I must say that I'll always love you sincerely

My Darling Wife

How sweet it is to wake up every day beside you
Knowing you'll be there for me in whatever I do
Hearing your voice is the sweetest thing to me
It helps me to face the world and all of its miseries
Coming home to you, is the turning point of my life
And I can't wait to be loving you, my darling wife
It's very poignant whenever I leave you for a day
And to be with you for always is for what I pray
Wherever I go without you is torturing to me
And all I can feel is pain and misery
Your love is my lifeline as far as I can see
And beside you forever is where I want to be
I love you sincerely and this is true
And I hope you feel the same way too

I'M LEFT IN MISERY

It happened again last night
I felt lost when I saw him holding you tight
You had once belonged to me
But I was a fool and I caused you misery
Now you're his to have and to hold
Now he's the man who is in full control
I see you, and I'm reminded of how stupid I've been
And I wish I had my life to live over again
I sit by myself at times and think of you
And to win you back, there's nothing I wouldn't do
I can't help but to think how happy he must be
Because he has you by his side continually
When you left, I thought everything would be fine
Now I see how stupid I was when you were mine
I took you for granted, and that's true
It seem something was more important than you
Now those are things I can't bare to see
Because you're no longer here with me
Now loving you is the most important thing to me
Even though I'm now left in misery

I'll Never Hurt You Again

I'm having nightmares over and over again
Regretting that I've caused you so much pain
I wasn't thinking when I did this to you
Now I'm hurting through and through
I know that you're hurting too
Because I've told you many times how much I love you
but when you needed me, I wasn't there
and I know you must be wondering, why is life so unfair
you're my woman and I forget to say
I wish you a happy Mother's day
And even on your birthday, it was if I didn't care
I know you needed me, but I wasn't there
What should I do
To make it up to you?
I know I do not want to get into a fight
And I know sorry doesn't always make it right
But if you give me another chance to ease your pain
I promise I'll never hurt you again

www.ingramcontent.com/pod-product-compliance
Lightning Source LLC
Chambersburg PA
CBHW032216040426
42449CB00005B/618